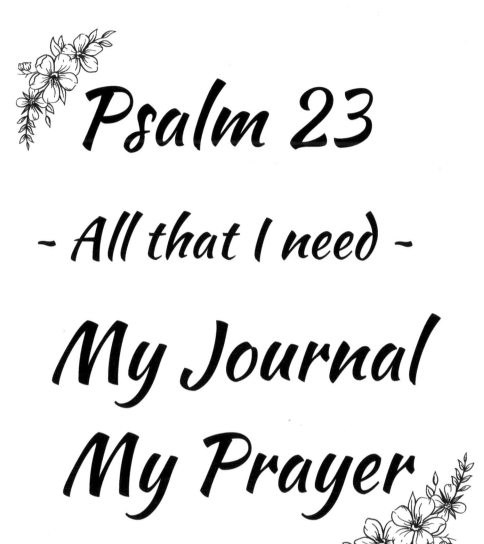

Psalm 23

- All that I need -

My Journal
My Prayer

PowerJournaling

Psalm 23
- All that I need -
My Journal
My Prayer

PowerJournaling

Published by HNI Books

ISBN: 978-0-9993905-4-2

As I step out in faith to put this journal in your hands, my hope is you will take action by reading and thinking about Psalm 23. Then let your thoughts, feelings, questions, concerns and prayers pour out on the page.

You also are stepping out in faith—seeking connection with God. I have no doubt you will be blessed when you take action. God's Word is powerful. When you focus on it, meditate on it, memorize it, pray it, speak it, write, draw, or dwell on it, it transforms you.

This journal is your safe place. Contemplate this psalm and get everything out on the page. Use color and doodles, highlighters, photos, crayons … whatever you like.

Choose your favorite Bible--maybe NIV, NLT, or The Message. Read & refer to the suggested Scriptures as you contemplate Psalm 23. Then return to this journal with your feelings, musings, and prayers. It's your safe place.

Don't be surprised if the Spirit nudges you, or a revelation or brilliant idea comes to mind. Nothing is too crazy to put on the page. This is your safe place. And perhaps a springboard to a new life.

Your Shepherd is here with you. Now and Always.

His Power is in your heart and hands. Choose your color and go.

The Twenty Third Psalm

The Lord is my shepherd; I shall not want.

He maketh me to lie down in green pastures:
he leadeth me beside the still waters.

He restoreth my soul:
he leadeth me in the paths of righteousness
for his name's sake.

Yea, though I walk
through the valley of the shadow of death,
I will fear no evil:
for thou art with me;
thy rod and thy staff they comfort me.

Thou preparest a table before me
in the presence of mine enemies:
thou anointest my head with oil;
my cup runneth over.

Surely goodness and mercy shall follow me
all the days of my life:
and I will dwell in the house of the Lord for ever.

The Lord is my shepherd; I shall not want.

Thank You, Lord,
You take my hand
and guide me.
I have all
that I need.

I'm grateful for...

I have all that I need...

He maketh me to lie down in green pastures:
he leadeth me beside the still waters.

Thank You, Lord, You watch over
my life & protect me
Psalm 121

He maketh me to lie down in green pastures:
he leadeth me beside the still waters.

Thank You, Lord, Your Grace pours on
me. You fight the battle & I rest in You
Exodus 14:14

He maketh me to lie down in green pastures:
he leadeth me beside the still waters.

Lord, I trust You & I rely on You.
Thank You, for Your provision!

How has God provided a safety net for me?

He restoreth my soul:
he leadeth me in the paths of righteousness
for his name's sake.

How has Jesus invited me to follow Him?

Jesus, The Bread of Life, can fulfill ALL our needs.
How has "bread" symbolized provision?

Jesus, The Bread of Life
John 6:35-40

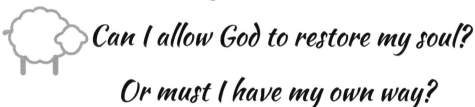

He restoreth my soul:
he leadeth me in the paths of righteousness
for his name's sake.

Can I decide each day, each moment, to be led by God?

Can I allow God to restore my soul?

Or must I have my own way?

God's Will or my will?

Jesus said, "I am the way and the truth and the life.
No one comes to the Father except through me."
John 14:6

He restoreth my soul:
he leadeth me in the paths of righteousness
for his name's sake.

My Soul = My Mind + My Will + My Emotions

Can I put my mind, my will, my emotions,

MY LIFE, in God's hands?

Or must I have my own way?

How has my will, my way, worked for me?

He restoreth my soul:
he leadeth me in the paths of righteousness
for his name's sake.

Can I find my true self, my identity, in Jesus?

Read, ponder, write about Romans 8.
<u>*NOTHING*</u> *can separate me from the Love of God!*

Jesus said, "I have come that they may have life,
and have it to the full."
John 10:10

He restoreth my soul:
he leadeth me in the paths of righteousness
for his name's sake.

Doodles, drawings, words, thoughts & prayers...

Jesus said, "Do not let your hearts be troubled.
Trust in God; trust also in me."
John 14:1

He restoreth my soul:
he leadeth me in the paths of righteousness
for his name's sake.

I follow Jesus, my Shepherd
I'm stepping out in faith

I'm grateful for
Your Blessings,
Lord

Counting my
Blessings

Praising
the Lord

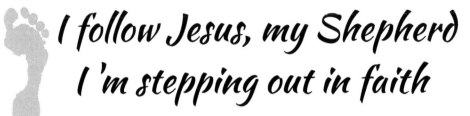

He restoreth my soul:
he leadeth me in the paths of righteousness
for his name's sake.

I follow Jesus, my Shepherd
I'm stepping out in faith

Steps that come to mind ...

Jesus said, "My sheep listen to my voice..."
John 10:27

He restoreth my soul:
he leadeth me in the paths of righteousness
for his name's sake.

I follow Jesus, my Shepherd
I'm stepping out in faith

Blessings I am asking for...

The Fruit of The Spirit

Love

Joy

Peace

Patience

Kindness

Goodness

Faithfulness

Gentleness

Self-Control

Galatians 5:22

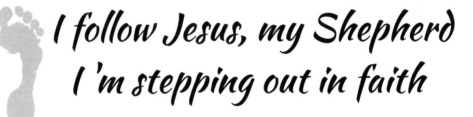

He restoreth my soul:
he leadeth me in the paths of righteousness
for his name's sake.

I follow Jesus, my Shepherd
I'm stepping out in faith

Blessings I have recieved...
Blessings I am asking for...

Doodles, drawings, words, thoughts & prayers

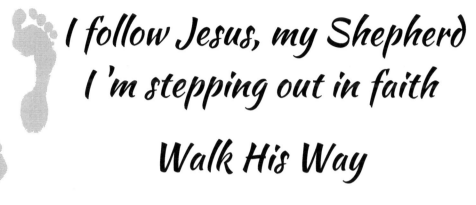

He restoreth my soul:
he leadeth me in the paths of righteousness
for his name's sake.

I follow Jesus, my Shepherd
I'm stepping out in faith

Walk His Way

Love God ... Love People

What does Obedience to God look like for me?

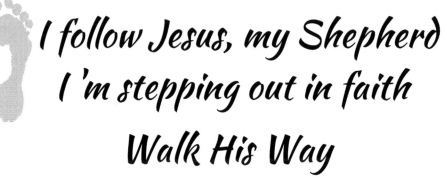

He restoreth my soul:
he leadeth me in the paths of righteousness
for his name's sake.

I follow Jesus, my Shepherd
I'm stepping out in faith
Walk His Way

How can I love God better?

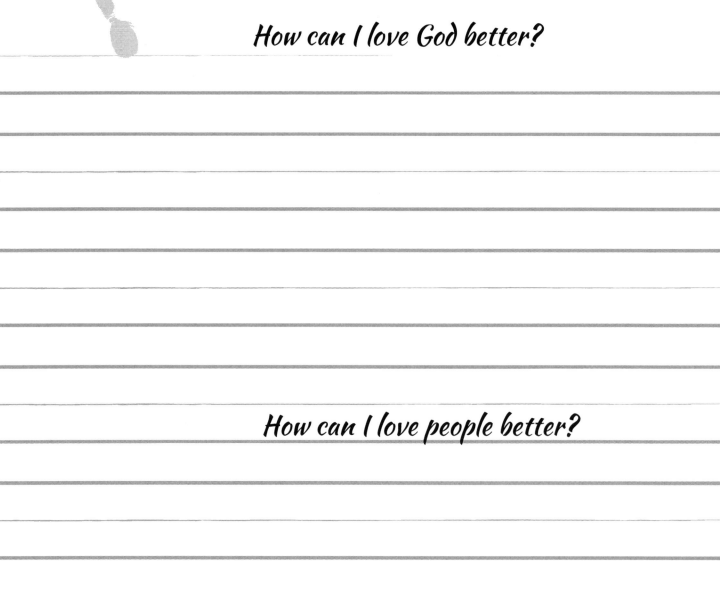

How can I love people better?

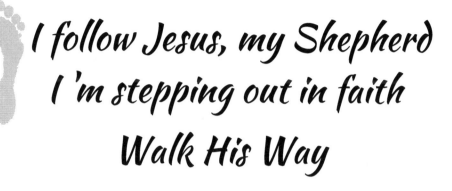

He restoreth my soul:
he leadeth me in the paths of righteousness
for his name's sake.

I follow Jesus, my Shepherd
I'm stepping out in faith
Walk His Way

How can I love people better?

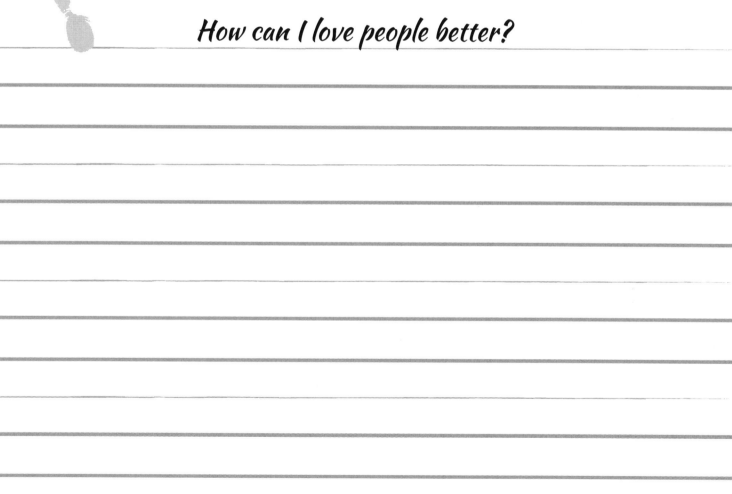

Live by the Spirit! ... Galatians 5
Pour out your thoughts & prayers

He restoreth my soul:
he leadeth me in the paths of righteousness
for his name's sake.

Walk His Way

How can I love people better?

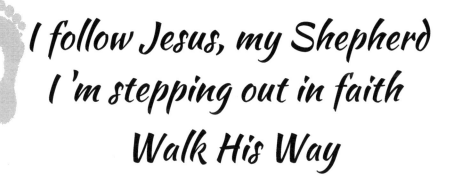

He restoreth my soul:
he leadeth me in the paths of righteousness
for his name's sake.

I follow Jesus, my Shepherd
I'm stepping out in faith
Walk His Way

Who do I need to forgive?

Prayer & Forgiveness ... Matthew 6:9-15
Pour out your thoughts & prayers

He restoreth my soul:
he leadeth me in the paths of righteousness
for his name's sake.

Walk His Way
Who do I need to forgive?

He restoreth my soul:
he leadeth me in the paths of righteousness
for his name's sake.

Walk His Way

Doodles, drawings, words, thoughts & prayers...

Yea, though I walk
through the valley of the shadow of death,
I will fear no evil:
for thou art with me;
thy rod and thy staff they comfort me.

FEAR is False Evidence Appearing Real
What am I afraid of?

Yea, though I walk
through the valley of the shadow of death,
I will fear no evil:
for thou art with me;
thy rod and thy staff they comfort me.

How has Fear stopped me?

Doodles, drawings, words, thoughts & prayers...

Yea, though I walk
through the valley of the shadow of death,
I will fear no evil:
for thou art with me;
thy rod and thy staff they comfort me.

Perfect

LOVE

Drives Out Fear
1John 4:18

Doodles, drawings, words, thoughts & prayers...

*Yea, though I walk
through the valley of the shadow of death,
I will fear no evil:
for thou art with me;
thy rod and thy staff they comfort me.*

*Jesus said not to worry...
Read, ponder, write about Matthew 6:25-34*

Doodles, drawings, words, thoughts & prayers...

Yea, though I walk
through the valley of the shadow of death,
I will fear no evil:
for thou art with me;
thy rod and thy staff they comfort me.

I hand over my Fear to God.
I have peace beyond understanding.

Rejoice & read Philippians 4 ... powerful paragraphs!

Doodles, drawings, words, thoughts & prayers...

Yea, though I walk
through the valley of the shadow of death,
I will fear no evil:
for thou art with me;
thy rod and thy staff they comfort me.

God gives me peace beyond understanding.

I'm thinking about Whatever is...
True
Noble
Right
Pure
Lovely
Admirable
Excellent
Praiseworthy

Phil. 4:8

Yea, though I walk
through the valley of the shadow of death,
I will fear no evil:
for thou art with me;
thy rod and thy staff they comfort me.

Thinking about God's goodness & power...

True

Noble

Right

Pure

Lovely

Admirable

Excellent

Praiseworthy

Doodles, drawings, words, thoughts & prayers...

Yea, though I walk
through the valley of the shadow of death,
I will fear no evil:
for thou art with me;
thy rod and thy staff they comfort me.

God's promise:
I will never leave you or forsake you.
Joshua 1:5, 9

Doodles, drawings, words, thoughts & prayers...

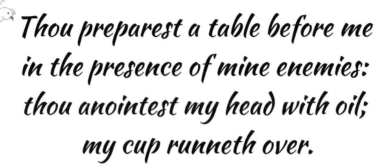

Thou preparest a table before me
in the presence of mine enemies:
thou anointest my head with oil;
my cup runneth over.

How has God prepared my table?
Saved by Grace ... Romans 5 &6

Doodles, drawings, words, thoughts & prayers...

Thou preparest a table before me
in the presence of mine enemies:
thou anointest my head with oil;
my cup runneth over.

God's grace is all we need.
In our weakness, He is strong
2 Corinthians 12:9

thou anointest my head with oil

I invite the Holy Spirit in daily.
I walk in the Spirit & enjoy the
Fruit of the Spirit.

Holy Spirit & the Fruit of the Spirit
Luke 11:13 & Galatians 5:22

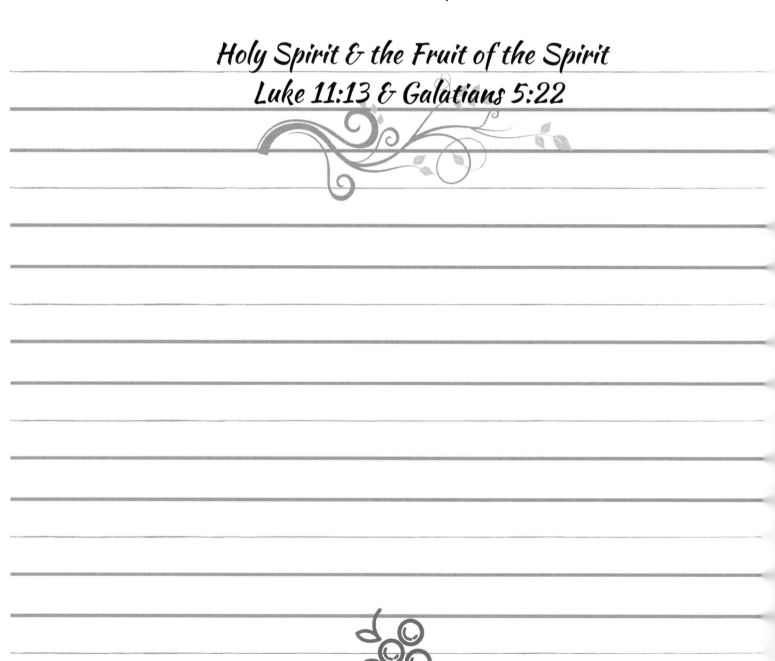

thou anointest my head with oil

I invite the Holy Spirit in daily.
I walk in the Spirit & enjoy the
Fruit of the Spirit.

Read, ponder, write about John 15
Jesus is the vine...we are the branches

thou anointest my head with oil

I invite the Holy Spirit in daily.
I walk in the Spirit & enjoy the
Fruit of the Spirit.

Read, ponder, write about John 15
Jesus invites us to REMAIN

thou anointest my head with oil

I invite the Holy Spirit in daily.
The Spirit renews my mind.

Renew & Transform ... Romans 12:2
Pour out your thoughts & prayers...

thou anointest my head with oil

I invite the Holy Spirit in daily.

God's Holy Presence lives in me.

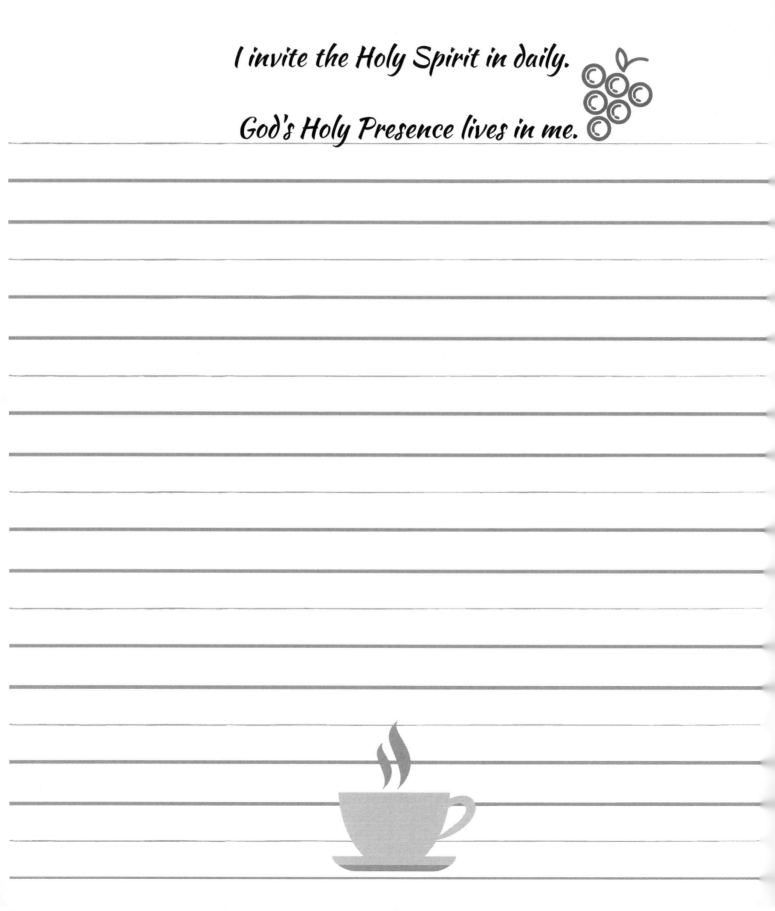

My cup runneth over!

Doodles, drawings, words, thoughts & prayers...

My cup runneth over!

Let Go
&
Live in
God's Grace!

Doodles, drawings, words, thoughts & prayers...

My cup runneth over!

LOVE

Surely goodness and mercy shall follow me
all the days of my life:
and I will dwell in the house of the Lord for ever.

Let Go & Live in
God's Grace!

Surely goodness and mercy shall follow me
all the days of my life:
and I will dwell in the house of the Lord for ever.

Can I let go of my need to control
and let God take care of me?

Let Go & Live in
God's Grace!

Surely goodness and mercy shall follow me
all the days of my life:
and I will dwell in the house of the Lord for ever.

Can I let go and Trust God for
provision? For all my needs?

Let Go & Live in God's Grace!

Surely goodness and mercy shall follow me
all the days of my life:
and I will dwell in the house of the Lord for ever.

God's Grace is unearned favor,
loving kindness

Let Go & Live in
God's Grace!

Surely goodness and mercy shall follow me
all the days of my life:
and I will dwell in the house of the Lord for ever.

God's Mercy is unearned forgiveness

Let Go & Live in
God's Grace!

Surely goodness and mercy shall follow me
all the days of my life:
and I will dwell in the house of the Lord for ever.

I need only make the choice...

Let Go & Live in God's Grace!

Surely goodness and mercy shall follow me
all the days of my life:
and I will dwell in the house of the Lord for ever.

Lord, let me be a conduit of Your Grace...

Let Go & Live in
God's Grace!

The Twenty Third Psalm

The Lord is my shepherd; I shall not want.

He maketh me to lie down in green pastures:
he leadeth me beside the still waters.

He restoreth my soul:
he leadeth me in the paths of righteousness
for his name's sake.

Yea, though I walk
through the valley of the shadow of death,
I will fear no evil:
for thou art with me;
thy rod and thy staff they comfort me.

Thou preparest a table before me
in the presence of mine enemies:
thou anointest my head with oil;
my cup runneth over.

Surely goodness and mercy shall follow me
all the days of my life:
and I will dwell in the house of the Lord for ever.

The Lord is
my shepherd;
I shall not want.

The Lord is
my shepherd;
I have all that I need.

1

He maketh me
to lie down in
green pastures:
he leadeth me beside
the still waters.

2

He restoreth my soul:
he leadeth me
in the paths of
righteousness
for his name's sake.

3

Yea, though I walk
through the valley of
the shadow of death,
I will fear no evil:
for thou art with me;
thy rod and thy staff
they comfort me.

4

Thou preparest a
table before me
in the presence
of mine enemies:
thou anointest
my head with oil;
my cup runneth over.

5

Surely goodness
and mercy
shall follow me
all the days of my life:
and I will dwell in
the house of the Lord
for ever.

6

The Fruit of The Spirit

Love

Joy

Peace

Patience

Kindness

Goodness

Faithfulness

Gentleness

Self-Control

Galatians 5:22

The Fruit of The Spirit
Love
Joy
Peace
Patience
Kindness
Goodness
Faithfulness
Gentleness
Self-Control
Galatians 5:22

Let Go
&
Live in
God's Grace!

Whatever is...
True
Noble
Right
Pure
Lovely
Admirable
Excellent
Praiseworthy
Phil 4:8

Walk
His
Way

CONGRATULATIONS!

You've completed your journal.

Continue to walk with your Shepherd day by day...

Let Go & Live in God's Grace

-All we need-

ABOUT THE AUTHOR

Paula M. Scully has journaled as long as she can remember. Her earliest included renditions of her favorite horses and simple stories about them. Later, journaling would sometimes turn to novel writing, blogs, and creating her own journals.

More recently, topics revolve around scripture and how God is (or seems not to be) moving in her life. Basically, conversations with God—prayer. In short, journaling has been one of her greatest pleasures, as well as one of the best ways to "do" life.

Power Journaling was her first published book, followed by two motivational "power journals" for kids of all ages. As Maeve Christopher, she has published eight novels. Her most recent series, *The Golden Bowl*, were international Amazon Best Sellers.

After recovering from a serious illness, Paula put her healthcare background (DMD, MBA) and interests in research and writing to work for FoodFaithWellness.com "A Novel Approach to Health & Wellness." She shares her insights and brings together information and inspiration to help others on their own personal journey.

Psalm 23, long one of her favorites, was a part of her journey to recovery, by the grace of God. Paula's experience, and an email from her editor expressing how much Maeve's novel had impacted her prayer life, reignited Paula's enthusiasm to write journals again.

She offers a simple invitation to join her in journaling to transform: Choose your color and go!

A NOTE FROM PAULA...

I'd love to hear from you. Tell me about your journaling journey. What did you like best? What did you experience?

If you enjoyed journaling through
Psalm 23 ~ All that I Need ~
I'd be honored if you would tell others by leaving a review on the site where you purchased this journal.

Email me:
paula@FoodFaithWellness.com
to share your experience

Visit:
https://FoodFaithWellness.com/Power-Journaling
to get access to the latest news,
journals and more from
Paula and Power Journaling

MORE...

From Maeve Christopher:
The Golden Bowl Series
A Ring and a Prayer
The Supernatural Diet Club
Tickets
For information and links to retailers visit:
MaeveChristopher.com

Coming Soon from Power Journaling:
Your Golden Bowl
a Prayer Journal inspired by
The Golden Bowl series
Visit:
https://FoodFaithWellness.com/Power-Journaling
to get access to the latest news,
journals and more from
Paula and Power Journaling

Made in the USA
Middletown, DE
25 October 2020